From Darkness to Light

Finding Your Inner Child

Cheryl Lunar Wind
and Friends

From Darkness to Light

Finding Your Inner Child

Any Inquiries contact:

cheryl.hiller@yahoo.com

Some of the poems in this collection first appeared in We Are One, Follow the White Rabbit, I Love Life, Know Your Way, Blessings Beyond Belief, Let It Be, Crossroads of Change, and Earth Almanac 2025 chapbooks; and on facebook.

Cover art credit to Brenda Gamache, 2026

Cover design credit to Rene Moraida, 2026

First edition.

Published by Alexander Agency Books,

Mount Shasta, California 96067

ISBN 979-8-9988971-5-3

From Darkness to Light

Finding Your Inner Child

Dedicated to David Brian Walas
April 19, 1953 -- November 23, 2025
whose life exemplified childlike joy.

Preface

We are all children at heart--
let us return to that state.
Jesus said "to become as little children".

Hopscotch, Hot Potato and do the Hokey Pokey.
Rock, Paper, Scissors.

What's your game?
Ever dream you can fly?
Leap over tall buildings,
Swing on a web like Spiderman...
Be fun & fancy-free.

These things will bring
Restoration & Fulfillment
of our purpose, path and way.

Inner Child Restoration--The Return of Original Frequency

"Beneath every emotional trigger lives a younger version of you that learned to adapt instead of feel safe.

The inner child is not a psychological metaphor--it is a living energetic imprint. When neglected, it manifests as fear, control, insecurity or emotional shutdown. When restored, it becomes creativity, intuition, joy and resilience.

A healed inner child creates a stable nervous system allowing coherence and ascension energy to anchor in the body. Innocence is not fragility but clarity without distortion."
---*online source*

This collection highlights personal examples of healing and reconnection with the inner child and reminds us to embrace joy by "becoming as young children".

Many thanks to all the contributors online and locally.

Contents

Darkness Into Light
by Anna Scheving

In the dark womb of mother earth
deep rest engulfs me.

Silence hums the eternal now
opening divine portals of wisdom within.

At last,
a flash of the grand cosmic mystery is revealed
and I surrender to it.

Darkness
by Linda Groszyk

where light can shine
go inside
depths
ready to be revealed
shadows
listen
understand
resonate
be with
hold
move through
scream
let go
quiet
stillness
openness
cuddle
attune
kiss
hold
love
embrace

A Message from the Lyran White Heart
by Rune Darling

.

We Have Descended
In Humble Might
To Bring Wisdom
Through Infinite Light

.

Arrived with a Purpose
Hearts to Elevate
Harmony Now Woven
Where All Souls Reside

.

A Message of Unity
From Worlds Where
The Echoes of Christ
Consciousness Hum

.

We Will Now Show
And Bring Forth
A Vision of what
You can Become

.

Hearts Outstretched
In a Gesture Kind
We Whisper of Oneness
Our Collective Hearts Intertwined

.

For Every Illusion
Darkness has Spun
We Will Shine Bright
Remembering
We All Are The One

.

So Let Us
Together Awaken
To the Call of Our Mother Star

.

Together We Rise and Transcend
In the Cosmic Dance Of Existence
Where New Beginnings Have No Ends

.

In the Heart of Humanity
A New Dawn Takes Flight
With Us the Lyrans from Lyra
Lets in Togetherness
Embrace the Light
.

Abundance
by Linda Groszyk

food
treasures
water
air
nature
community
BREATH
space
movement
time
LOVE
giving
sharing
connection

Friendship
by Linda Groszyk

being with
laughter
connection
allowing
accepting
seeing
listening
understanding
joy

Portal Play Time
by Cheryl

I am a space holder for Peace.

Otter Woman says--
Come swim in the cosmic ocean.

Return to Innocence

You are only as safe
as you think you are.

The animal & plant kingdoms
have been waiting for
the sons & daughters of men
to join in the fun.

Restoration is possible--
by being calm
carrying peace
softening your hearts & minds.

Gently down the stream--
We go.
No more fighting--
just adjust your frequency.

Free Spirit
by Anna Scheving

In Innocence, I leave my mother's dark womb.
Through Innocence, I experience the new light of dawn.

Even now, 56 years around the sun, whether in
darkness or in light, I choose to feel the Universe
as the vibration of Innocence.

In this moment I choose to connect with my trusting,
joyful inner child.
With no energies to block this creative, intuitive flow,
my spirit soars into dimensions beyond my critical mind,
bringing clarity and peace.

Aho

Rainbows
by Linda Groszyk

softness
special
colors
surprises
light
delight
glee
sky
breath
inhale
exhale
beingness. . . .

Where Dreams Come True
by Cheryl

On the Merry-Go-Round of Life---
Up and Down,
Round and Round

Here we go---

Take a Leap--
Dive deep--

Hold your breath--
Squeeze your eyes shut--
Tight--

Jump
down the wormhole---

To the rainbow
play with Peter Pan--
in Never Never Land.

On the Merry-Go-Round of Life---
I'm gonna ride
all nite long.

The strong wind blows--
to the rainbow--
where dreams come true.

Catch
the next train to Georgia---
Follow the birds
Fly south for the winter.

Past the smog--
You'll find a city in the sky--
Never Never Land
where dreams come true.

Have you lost your way?
Shut your eyes--
hold your breath--

Pull the plug
go down the drain.
Ride the wind

Round and Round
We go
On the Merry-Go-Round of Life.

Being Joy
by Cheryl

The portal of the Sacred heart brings--
Safety, Clarity, & Calm

The Original mind is--
Child-like, Pure & Innocent
Restorative.

I am a leader of light.
A space holder for peace.
I'm here to assist and bless all mankind.

A recipe for Joy--
Soften your thoughts.
Be gentle with yourself.
Accepting, Allowing.
Being Joy.

Oceanic Alchemy
by Shivrael

I can do this hard thing
And strip away the layers of adulthood
To the pure essence underneath.

The Otter People wish
To come play with me.
They meet me in the etheric spaces
Along with my higher self
Who offers me medicine
For my transformation.

She invites me to wade into
The cosmic ocean of consciousness.
I see her in the form of a goddess of the sea,
Cocha Mama, the Ocean Mother
And also as Yemaya, spirit of the water.

She calls me to submerge myself fully
In her living, healing waters
Offering cleansing and purification,
Stripping me to my pure essence
So that I remember the innocence of being.

Something softens in this oceanic alchemy.
I let go
And become childlike and fully healed.

Spirit always has answers.
All it takes is asking for help,
And it is given.
Enter the liminal space
Between the worlds
With imagination and meditation,
Finding peace and clarity once again.
Thank you Great Spirit.

Traversing Troubling Times
by Cheryl

When your walking
On a steep bridge
made of rope, wood slats under your feet,
Swaying in the wind---
Don't look down.
Look straight ahead.
Keep your eye simple---
Your focus pure--
Straight Forward.
Your thoughts will take
you where you want to go.

It's always been you
and the U-N-I-V-E-R-SE.

Anything else is a distraction.
So keep going,
You got this.

V.I.B.E.
by Elizabeth Carrillo

In hallowed heart space with clear intention
In Muladhara an ancient rhythm starts
In breath, in hum, in drum, sacred belly wakes
Out of voice and body in collective to find

V.I.B.E.
Vibration...Intention... Breath... Exhale

Ahhh...the chest opening begins, it's reconnecting clear
A vibration warming the ears, crystal clear
Resonating deep, lungs with plexus fire now clear
The tension breaks with a joyful hum...you hear?

V.I.B.E.
Vibration...Intention... Breath... Exhale

Uuuu... the Vishuddha awakens to catch the wave
A trembling yet grounded, sensual, powerful wave
A bridge through unconditional Anahata love wave
Releasing that which that old mind tries to save

V.I.B.E.
Vibration...Intention... Breath... Exhale

Mmmm...the true eye flares in colorful rings
Jaw unclenched, cosmic ocean in aqua aura rings
Softening shoulders, restored safety in crown that rings
Then head rush, toe rush... everything in between

With all of Being to become now in childlike play
With nowhere left for fear to hide, it transmutes
With pure coherence abounding from soul to skin
Within, the outer would is attuned

Double Date
by Cheryl

Double take--
take to make

spin a yarn
tell a tale--fib
just a little white lie
(make an impression)

Double dip
Double meaning

Chinese checkers--rolling, running away
Chinese fire drill---
In and Out

Double dutch
skip along

Double date--
double trouble

Double take--
Do it again.

Name that Tune
by Cheryl

Up, down,
Clown around

Here, there, where?

Cause--
cause & effect.

Why?

Because.

Love fiercely--
go gently into the nite.

Winning, Loosing--

Calling, Stalling--

Naming, Gaming

Play the Game of Life!

Life Is a Game
by Cheryl

At the House of cards----
You can...
    Take a chance
    Roll the dice
    Find true love.

Play the game of Life
on the Earth board.
Level Up!
Live, Learn and Love.

My Inner Child
by Chris Johns

I hear him sometimes.
In fact, I am him at times—
that beautifully broken,
terrified little child
still whispering
from the corners of my mind.

The one who never felt
like he belonged.
Who learned to stay quiet,
to smile through the riot,
pretending he was fine
while dying inside it.

The boy who learned to pray
in all the right ways,
yet felt only
his insides decay.

I feel him still—
in the sorrow,
in the trembling ache
of silence gone hollow.
When the night grows heavy
and my chest turns to stone,
he crawls from the shadow
to remind me
I am not alone.

I hear him mutter
through my voice,
stutter through the choice
of words I dare not speak aloud—
truth buried
to remain proud.

I return to this place often—
not to dwell,
but to remember

the putrid scent of fear
and self-abandonment
that created my hell.

I whisper softly,
“It’s over now.
We made it somehow.”
But still he weeps—
through my dreams,
through my seams,
through every mask
hiding luminous beams.

Sometimes he laughs—
a ghost in the glass,
mocking the man
who swore he’d outgrown
what still burns
from his past.

And yet…
in that laughter,
I hear grace—
a strange mercy
in the face
of pain too sacred
to erase.

So I let him breathe.
I let him bleed.
I let him need.
And when he fades,
I feel him stay—
beneath my ribs,
where suffering and grace
intertwine.

Not broken.
Not whole.
Just mine.

Starchild
by Shivrael

My magical child within
Wants to play and be in joy.
I know she holds the key
On this holy portal day.
She believes in unicorns
And magic
When the rest of me
Has gotten too serious,
worrying over adult things.
She says, "Let that go."
And I listen.
Purging my ego's concerns
Feels entirely useful
As I find the hidden road of happiness
Stretching over deserts.

There, a jack rabbit
Sees me with shiny eyes
Hopping powerfully
To the great beyond.
I follow toward what lies ahead.

Listening to the North Star
by Shivrael

The alchemy of my inner world-
It is an entire constellation
That lives inside my heart.
The high heart
Is the North Star
Of my being.

Transmutation
by Shivrael

I am going to stand with my inner child
as we allow this wave
of ripples in the fabric
of my emotional body to pass.
I AM a soothing presence
to my Self
with the bigger whole of me
connected to Source and eternity.
This is a firefly's flash,
a moment in my life
in which the river of emotion flows.
At this moment, I show up
for my younger self
who is crying
and she doesn't know why.
I hold space for her
as the ripple passes through.
A tsunami of emotion
reaches the shores of my being
and I know that we are now
on the other side.
“Feeling is healing”
I remind her, my younger self.
She bravely allows herself
to feel it all
even if she feels scared.
Energy flows again,
and then she is
on the other side.
The witnessing of her feelings
is what is healing her.
She is on the mend,
soon to be laughing.
It makes me smile
to know that my medicine
of pure presence
has done it's magic
and that she and I will be o.k.
once again.

Dandelions and Daffodils
by Jennifer Hershelman

Blessings child, we are with you,
You have been very brave
Overcoming
Becoming
Transforming
the fears you've faced
into Gentle Strength

The white dove of Peace
flies with the healing winds
you have helped to put into place.

Mother Earth is anew & abounds
with unlimited creativity & opportunities
to move forward.

We have passed the Threshold--
the times of old have been laid to rest.

It is up to you to see it through.

What kind of world do you want to create?

The birds sing of patience,
as the winds bring healing and gentle guidance,
the waters murmur to themselves of all the great surprises,
the earth, the dirt and the trees hold us steady
as the chaos of change winds down.

The unicorns release bubbles of inspiration
for those still feeling stuck.

Watch out for the gnomes,
for though they are great guides and builders of/for our new paths,
they are mischievous with a very big sense of humor.

The crows stand watch keeping our energies protected, none shall
pass--any whom try to keep us from our path.

The leaders are being reminded who really rules the land.

So listen to the forest.
Embrace your inner child
& Go dance, sing and play!

Create the new world this DAY.

Childhood
by Kazi Ayaz Mahesar

I remember
Your village
By its trees
Your fragrance
By its roses

I remember
Your childhood
By its innocence
Your smiles
By their sobs

I remember
Your dreams
By your eyes
Your heart
By your longing

I remember
Your hopes
By your fears
Your joys
By your tears

I remember You
Do you;
Remember, Me?

I am walking
Syne eons
Beside you

I am your childhood
Your innocence,
See me; in you

And let's go
To the trees
We remember!

Running to Trees
by Kazi Ayaz Mahesar

Remember!
When we ran to trees

To touch--and
Run back to finish line

You
Always made it there first

Remember!
The day I did not return?

You were running,
Not seeing you were alone

Competing
With no one, but; yourself!

I smiled; as I sat
You could not win without me

And I,
Could not lose without you!

Remember?
How you longed to see me!

And I,
Kept hiding away

To the Truth
Of knowing, who I am!

Childhood Smoke
by Cheryl

Are we like the flowers---
beautiful,
fragile yet strong
at the same time?
As we get older,
does the world get colder?
Like a song,
that passes too quickly?

When your mother tells you that your dad doesn't love you---
When your step-dad kicks your cat and tells you how good you look----
When you can't breathe
because of all the ciggarette butts laying around---
Its
Childhood Smoke.

I remember chasing wild kittens in my Grandma's barn.
I found a 4-leaf clover that day,
and I knew all would be well.

Please, Please Momma,
don't drive so fast.

I gave my mom a hard time,
Coming,
After 3 days of labor---
Out I came, feet first---
It was like,
I knew what I was in for,
And, I had changed my mind.

The story is that my mom
threw me, as a newborn,
Perhaps I just slipped off the couch---
But my grandmother took care of me.
She was an angel,
Who now, still helps me
from her place, on the other side.

One day, my mom packed up my stuff
and dropped me off
at my dad's house---
soon after,
I woke up with his hands around my throat---

I don't know what's worse---
Not being loved by my dad---
Or being loved too much by my stepdad.

I grew up watching Gilligen's Island---
If those seven strangers could get along
on a deserted island,
then why couldn't we?

Round and Round, we go.
For a three hour tour, we go.

Where is the love and light?
We are.
We create,
by living our lives.
In fact, that is why we are here.
We are one,
of the many threads,
in this tapestry of life.

Look back to that 4-leaf clover,
We are never alone, and
We are loved.

The angels are singing---
Look at that Cheryl---
She took Childhood Smoke,
and turned it into Light.

Magic Carpet Style Ride
by Mary Krkljus

Occasional looks outside
Why do some days just float by?

Raising of the blinds
Watering of the plants
Coffee's been made
Time to dance!

Sort through what we need to do
Waiting for the mail
Trying not to come unglued

Much to do in this dance with time
Start to hum, formulate a rhyme
Before I even know
What comes next
It's gotten dark

Like a witches hex on time
Suddenly, I'm lowering the blinds

As I roll my eyes
With a silent giggle
Loosening my hips with a slight wiggle

I begin to gear up
As I sit up, straightening my spine
Seeing how it really should be in a straight line...
With a slight curve I turn,
I peek through the blinds..
It's confirmed it's night time.

As I take off "magic carpet" style Ride
Dreaming of the days that are hidden inside
I begin to see the beauty of this dreamy ride.

Infinite magic carpet style Ride.

Avatar
by Mary Krkljus

Out of the fire I rise
No compromise
Just real eyes
Seeing crystal clear
Levels-equations-mismatches
About good and bad
Dark and Light
Often the dark teaches right
Leads to the light
Steering away from the ships
Of friends, family
Everything once known
Allows one to see
How they were overthrown
Through solidarity we find our crown
We must rise
Not sync with the ships
A real cookie has all the chips

Power Rangers
by Cheryl Lunar Wind

The Transformation Team
has arrived on Earth
like Power Rangers
We Five Meet
in circle--
We are a new collective.

Whirling Rainbow Anna--
her voice trascends time & space turning all that hear to rainbow stars.
"Indeed, O Peoples,
Whirling Stars of generous
Light and Song you'll be."

Greenie the Gold--
embodies helping rays by quoting the ancient mysteries, sacred geometries
and the nature spirits.

Violet Flame Fillup--
brings in practices of love, mercy and grace to planet Earth.

Cheryl White Wind--
blows out cobwebs with words of wisdom. She rides the rapids on the
White River of spirit.

Shivrael Blue Ray--
Shivrael carries galactic blessings and her angelic wand blesses all it touches.

They turn time on a dime---
and hail from the future, traveling
the Antakarana Bridge across galaxies.

Meeting in circle--
No longer
little people with daily troubles--
they Grow into More--

In a Flash--
they become bigger than the average human
able to move past any traumas or dramas.

Their superpowers are many and varied.
You may catch them,
playing that funky music,
creating sacred art,
holding space, offering a kind ear,
sharing angelic vibes
or galactic messages...

Their mission?
Transcend this world of doubt and fear--
Radiating Rainbow Rays of light.

**Greenie is quick to tell me that white isn't a color.
I am resistant to this information.
If I can see it---it is real.
More than that--I feel it, and I send it out--
an energy wave of the brightest purity.
Her face glows and smiles with green light.
Green means Go.

Fillup questions prophecy and Thoth gives him a message
and a symbol to remember.

Shivrael checks within her Sacred Library and tells us that our 'Eye of Understanding'
will open now as 3i Atlas comes closer than ever.

Rainbow Woman reminds us that All is One, Bringing rainbow energy to the group--
she knows many paths, many roads will all lead to the One.

We are all part of the great story.
We are a new collective--
twinkling stars,
volunteers on Ascending Earth.

Words- part one
by Cody Ray Richardson

Words don't use words
Words just are
It tells you something about words
We use them but they don't use us
Words are symbols
Do the sounds represent the symbols
Do the symbols represent the sounds
So many words for the same things
So many different languages
Different symbols and different sounds
They represent things that are different to different beings
Interesting enough when I was happy I had little words
Now that I'm not so happy I have many words
Words give the energy someplace to go
when I'm not able to be in coherence
with certain people or certain surroundings
Words give me a pathway back to coherence
They're more than just symbols and sounds
They are the pathway back to something that makes sense
When I write I am time traveling
I might read it years from now and understand what I did not know then
I'm speaking to others without knowing I am
I'm actually speaking to the words themselves
"Words please help me find a way
to meet the need I cannot seem to through others"
Please words help me back to love
Help me back to understanding
I know within you is the way back to her
I somehow misunderstand words at times
Sometimes words are portals to trauma
Sometimes words bring back memories
Words brought me to this place through misunderstanding
Through understanding hopefully I can see eye to eye with love again
I can see eye to eye with anyone again
At this point I think I might just be stranded on an island of words for now
Never able to really relate to any person
Never to get my needs met

Just riding in my writing
Like a snowboarder would hit the powder
Finding the fresh new words
Putting them in an order that they have never been before
The words themselves beckoning me for the next line
All timelines merging into the one that is being created now
I am a god when I write
I am free from pain
I'm free from my triggers
I'm free from what may or may not be manipulation
I will be careful about what I write

Victory
by Pradeep Nawarathna

The greatest victory
is not over others,
but over oneself.
To master desire,
to calm the mind,
to walk with peace—
this is accomplishment.

Light & Dark
by Pradeep Nawarathna

Light follows light,
and darkness fades.
Darkness hides in light,
waiting for fuel to end.
When light is gone,
darkness reigns again.
Yet even a spark
can break the night.

Truth
by Mercy Talley

We cannot reject The Truth
based on others misinterpretation
& flawed representation ~

The Truth Stands Eternal
and is not to be confused
with personal opinions ~

The Truth is True Law
& is etched within
Our Hearts & Bones ~

Cleansing, so we can
Hear Clearly, we then
Can Know The Truth ~

By Listening Within
we come into Fellowship
with The Creator of All That Is ~

Love is The Currency
upon which Life flows
Abundantly to All ~

With Eyes to See
Ears to Hear &
Hearts Willing to Know

U.S.S. Enterprise NCC-1701
by Rune Darling

.

We Will
BOLDLY GO
WHERE NO MAN
OR WOMAN HAS GONE BEFORE

.

.

Registry:
NCC-1701
Encoded at Launch

.

Class:
Classified with
Metaphysical Upgrades

.

Primary Directive:
Speak Truth

.

Secondary Directive:
Translate the Unknown

.

.

We Stand at The Edge
Of what is Known

.

Not to Conquer,
Not to Convince

.

We Choose
Curiosity Over Certainty
Listening Before Naming
Feeling Before Defining

.

We Accept Responsibility
For The Ground We Walk UpOn

.

We Do Not Demand Clarity
We Speak in Symbols

.

When The Path Dissolves
We Remain Present

When The Map Fails
We Trust Navigation
Over Destination
.
We Go First
So that No One
Has To Go Alone
.
This is Our Command.
This is Our Exploration
.
This is
Our Way

We Are Fully Galactic
by Shivrael

Cosmic blue light
Seeps into the consciousness
Of the Collective
Bringing the energy
Of awakening.

A Thunderbeing heralds change.
Eyes open with new ways
Of seeing through the veil.

The blue light from Source
Is a catalyst
Illuminating a new way
Of being.

Get on board this
Fast-moving spaceship
Carrying Earth's people
Into transformation.

Beings with heart-centered emanations
Are painting a new picture
Of the galaxy
Based on love and equality.
We have become fully galactic.

Sayings
by Mary Krkljus

I took comfort when I heard..
"We're all crazy"

I took action when I heard...
"When you feel like you hate yourself, take a shower'.

I got nervous when I heard..
"Cold shower water cleanses you of negativity".

I got inspired when I heard..
"Become what you love"

I had doubts when I heard...
"You are enough"

I felt strange relief when I heard...
"No one ever helped you cause you are the one you've been waiting for!"

I felt challenged when I desired to be self sufficient.
I've been exhausted doing it all.

Rain or shine, hot or cold, tired or not...
It's always on me.

It's exhausting but you know what?
There are no more sleepless nights!

So many years I relied on some magical pill from a doctor
for just about everything!

Now? I make myself figure it out!

It's about God, Water, movement, interest, joy, rhythm, music and self expression, nature, curiosity and a will to explore, to grow, to learn,
to understand...
We create our limitations and we can change that!

Counterparts
by Ember Coal

"We are not the same."

The Moon said to the Sun.

"Our alchemy dances like spectral waves. Soul strings are tied to each other, yet never reach. Never embracing. This is why our power was split, and why it must be obtained by the living."

"We are not the same."

The Moon rested her somber white head on a cloud and started to drift away.

"Yes. We are counterparts." The Sun replied.
Stopping the Moon's retreat.
"Counterparts can create, opposites can destroy. You speak of alchemy, but where is yours?"
The Sun in his brazenness challenged the Moon.

"You want to see alchemy?"
The Moon sat up, her white haze beginning to burn brighter with her soft milky light.

"Then take note and be wary. For I am the depths of the voided soul in which life must conquer before rising in the dawn. But, take haste, for my space is not for the weak. My shadows hold monsters of their own making. Realms in which living things must purge before my light shines upon them."
The Moon swayed and stars gently shifted, making way for her soft density.

"For I am the Light in the Void. The bridge of realms, the portal to new consciousness. For divinity to rise it must first learn how to rest in my shadows, how to transmute its monsters, and learn the names of its mistakes. My rotation is slow, intentional.
True growth must begin within the voided soul so it may know balance when it reaches your rays."

Standing at her tallest, the Moon watches the Sun.
Her own light radiates among the stars.

"We are not the same."
She taunts the Sun this time.
The Sun smiles, eagerly accepting the Moon's justified ego.

"Counterparts." The Sun states simply.
"Counterparts are the source of all matter. Our duality is a dance in which we must learn to weave. Without our entanglement life will cease to Ascend. Your words strike true, 'life must conquer'. To truly see the dawn life must first know its shadows."

The Sun stands firm against its counterpart.
"Although we are split and we have been made anew our eternity was written as such. Life. Renewed in shadows, birthed in light. For once they have learned how to balance us both, then they find solace in your shadows. A restful healing in the void. A peace among their monsters turned sunlight because they have embraced your bridge."

The Sun matches the Moon's height.
Not to overpower but to match.
"And I. I am the blazing force in which life must conquer next. I am the path written, the bright days ahead. I am the Fool within the Equilibrium. The Lovers reunited within, and I am the Dawn. Eager to rise and drag the weary from the ashes."

The Sun burns brighter, matching the Moon in her glory.
"So, you see, Counterparts.
Are you ready to rise with me?"

The Sun offers his hand, a gentle invitation and a challenge.
The Moon does not waver.

She accepts the Sun's invitation.

The Sun Wheel Turns
by Rune Darling

W∑ AR∑
Touched And Shown
In Ancient Lyran Stone
.
Soon It Will Be Known
That We Are Not Alone
.
Humanity
BeComes One Species
An Evolution of Consciousness
.
Golden Threads Of Solar Flares
Unifying Us In A Blink Of An Eye
As We Turn The Sun Wheel
A Pure and Clear Portal is Given
.
Sirius Our Portal Star
Aligns in a Cosmic Dance
Takes Flight With 13 Hearts in Trance
.
Time Folds
As Unity Sparks &
Ignites Our Diamond Soul
.
Tabula Rasa for All
In this New Year 2026
We Shall Both Rise & Fall
.
Darling
On The Rise

Tableau Rasa

by Shima Moore

Cold wet weather
grounding giant ancient trees
in sacred sovereignty.
Their mysterious magnificence
reflects the dark womb of shamanic bliss
Compassionate cycles,
a blank slate as we flow in divine chaos
entering the Age of Aquarius.
Infinity – still a Tableau Rasa
Even native wisdom
riddled with charlatans throughout the ages
now cleanses what is fake.
Hope and fear intermingle as the world wonders,
suddenly appearing 3iAtlas intrigues all through its cosmic rays.
We are witnesses and creators in Earth's quarter-century almanac
Poised,
ready to rekindle personal power and indigenous divinity.

Legume
by Xris Della Costa

Legitimate is the legume
that sits uncooked in a room
surrounded by oaken walls
Till one day the empire falls

The cast has no time to bow
when curtains fall from the stage
warriors take their vows
unraveled False Flags and charades

Impeccable like the lark
A bridge 'tween light and dark
Vigilant like an aardvark
Impermanent is the spark

Precipitous, the precipice
the old guard is on notice
Imminent is the collapse
as oligarchs lose their grasp

Marginalized are the meek
distracted, lazy and weak
for they shall inherit more debt
heeding puppets behind pulpits

Periodical cicadas hatch
brilliant blazes need but one match
We're reaching critical mass
start by evading tax

The Eye Of Providence
by Vivian Marie McIntosh

This planet will be inherited by the meek
Balance being the only treasure they seek

Ready to ride and to stand up to a fight
Proving their purpose, a powerful might

Facing disruptive situations and storms together
A family fortress withstanding any harsh weather

The Divine Humans are definitely returning
Here to give evilness it's very last warning

With them comes the Way of the Water
Willing to save sheep from the slaughter

Tapped into their God Given magic and gifts
Mending each one of Humanity's many rifts

Division and doubt only breed chaos and confusion
While unity and understanding rebirth a revolution

War and killing just brings more of the same
Protection is the name of this winning game

Where love and light drive out the dark hate
Higher frequencies can then lead to our fate

The big and the strong take care of the small
Be there with a calm heart whenever they fall

Not necessarily with physical strength and ability
Sometimes what's needed is wisdom and loyalty

Our greatest weakness is also our biggest strength
It's up to each of us to follow our faith in full length

ALL energy is borrowed and must be returned
Enjoy happy moments when they are earned

Embrace suffering as it shows itself on your path
Don't let it make you a victim or give into wrath

Just breathe, focus on your breath when you're blue
Build a bridge of consciousness to help you through

Heaven on Earth is why these warriors awoken
It's already here, like a word about to be spoken

A delightful dimension where compassion rules
Where the lips of knowledge are precious jewels

No place for ignorance or revenge in the New World
God's got the harpoon, now watch while it's hurled

Backward Compatibility
by Cheryl

In is Out--
Outside no longer matters.
We matter.
We create matter
from within.
Go inward--
For all healing, all activity and all matters.

All galaxies, universes, destinations
Are within.

Before, behind, afterwards
do we turn back?
You can never go back.
compare, combat, war--

Front porch or back door?
As humans--we cannot go backwards--
We learn by going forward--
(only time travelers move backwards)
As we move--
We grow, change and evolve--
Moving along the continuum.
Are we compatible with constant change?

It is a paradox.

Today, I am free from everything
by Cheryl

As the wave of everything ebbs and flows--
I release and let it all Go.

Don't know what tomorrow will bring--
Because it is all undecided--
the Universe is slippery that way.

All I have to do is show up.
Perhaps I'll invite some invisible friends
to come with.
We can play I Spy or talk to the animals
along the way.

But I am free from everything---
No expectations--
Good, bad or otherwise,
this is not the same as no hope--
It is total acceptance--
Whatever will be, will be.

Which way to go?
I do not know--
Hope for peaceful interactions--
Joyful relations--
But even so--
I can only speak for myself.

Finders Keepers
by Cheryl

When listening, I see
all I need
In seeing
I need nothing
Hearing everything
Holding nothing--

Not all things
are apparent--
Hidden--
Knowledge from within--
the eye of the Universe.

"I find to lose I lose to find."*

**with credit given to Kazi Ayaz Mahesar*
for inspiration and words in quotes

Here's one for the road
by Cheryl

What does it mean
when you pour your heart out
to someone?

Remember to keep some for yourself.

If you are always wanting to give to others,
but forget yourself
you will become depleted.

Self-love is the foundation
of all relationships.

If you have a friendship,
and are always giving--
but not receiving--
Check yourself.

Know you are deserving.

I AM
by Rune Darling

I AM
Soon
Standing
On the Mesa
Now Out of Time

Behold the 11th
Wonder of All There Is

A Dimensional Tear
A Third Shaking from Above
Now Reaching Us Below

Portals Shall Appear
As We Meet Our Fear
Realizing the Illusion

The Red, White & Blue
Kachinas are Coming through
Guiding & Melting Stone
To dissolve Our Fear

Flow Like Water they say
Keep your Heart & Mind Connected
Don't Astray---We Are Here to Stay

Pieces of the Cosmic Puzzle
Vibrating in Truth
Falling into Sacred Places
Lighting up Our Path as We Go

All I really want for Christmas
Is not just to Know
Because I AM
Like You
Here to Show

The Gift
by Cheryl

The nite was glorious, her
eyes brimming with stars--
Far off sounds
tickle awareness...
Her ship has finally come in.

Dreamcatcher-
shells and teal feathers dangling,
ancestor promise whispering

A thin long bird grins,
delivering packages of new life.

A fat man wearing red says wait-
there's more...
"Come for a ride in my sky chariot."

We journey through lifetimes, I see all my
choices- made and not made- some happy
some sad-
When we finished he said-
"Now it's up to you. Can you live with what you
saw and be at peace?"

That's the best Gift of all.

Heal Thyself
by Pradeep Nawarathna

Everyone is their own healer.
When you are well, you help others.
Peace inside makes every practice strong.
Pain inside can spread more pain.
So care for yourself with love.
Stay calm, stay steady, stay gentle.
From peace, you can do anything.
May all beings be happy and free.

Be the Bridge
by Pradeep Nawarathna

Free your heart from hate,
let kindness be your gate.
Free your mind of noise,
choose peace as your voice.
Simplify each day,
clear the clutter away.
Give love, expect less,
find wealth in selflessness.
Love more, shake the dirt,
turn wounds into worth.
In this life, be known—
as the bridge, not the stone.

Step Into Peace
by Lillian Poe

Quiet is the only way I can step into peace.
Acceptance also comes with quiet.

I have learned there are certain levels of quiet and it has become a security blanket I can put on. There are levels of peace, almost like a skin you can take off like a coat.

We become more powerful as we accept how powerful we are.
For me directing thoughts in peace helps us all.

This was a long, time-filled lesson that I am still learning.
We aren't supposed to be a planet of doers.
We are learning how to be beings.
The joy comes as we are being "What we choose".

12/21
by Cheryl

Me, Myself & I gathered
to party on the Solstice.

At the magic play house,
We wish upon a star,
and the little prince sings
a Lemurian Birthday song.

Light the candles--
Eat the cake--
and don't forget the spiced wine!

Let go of attachments--
We are all free will agents--

While a comet called Atlas speeds by,
Earth is rocked on her Axis.

Miss Minnie arrives to remind us not to be so serious.
My Christmas wish is for more days like this.

Back at ya
by Laurie Story Vela

You, yourself, and you
Gathered in my playhouse
With other friends
you and I invited

Your wishing star
joined the others in the
Wishing Star Jar
that still sits here holding wishes
and heart space fueled by Atlas

My voice and those of our
Lemurian ancestry--

joined the birthday song
started by the Little Prince

I baked the cake
and pulled out the candles
the Little Prince lit up
for you as we sang
to celebrate your light

I made the spiced wine
for us to sip
Someone grew the grapes
turned divine to grace our lips
I gifted you the unicorns
and the picture here of you adorned
Unicorn friends that also
welcomed Miss Minnie
in the circle of play we formed

Yes, we, us, all of us
Yes, me, my playhouse,
Yes, I can release attachment
to acknowledgment
Now that I have honored myself
I freely gave and will do so again
I am here to play and to celebrate
Life, and Love, and You, and All Unicorns

Play days are birthed in inspiration
fueled by preparation and dedication
There are and will be more play days
in the playhouse with playful souls
for it is the way of the unicorn

Rune's Song
by Malte

(Verse 1)
There goes a man with an open heart
with truth in his laugh
an honest friend who asks lovingly
until the facade falls in
He pokes softly but hits clean
so the veil falls off
a loving mirror, an honest look
that shows who we are

(Chorus)
For Rune took an IQ test
it said 69 - no stress at all
he's not smart about numbers and shit
he is wise - in the good old way
He laughs at rules, breaks system
see some truth in there

(Verse 2)
An angel in a man's disguise
walks amongst us here
a quantum magician with no sense of humor
but hits the spot - every time it happens
He says things without a smile
and the room is completely calm
for when Rune is serious
now we know the truth is on

(Chorus)
For Rune took an IQ test
it said 69 - no stress at all
he's not smart about numbers and shit
he is wise - in the good old way
He laughs at rules, breaks system
see some truth in there

(Verse 3 - Scary Verse)
He moves fast in his whole body
and yells out loud a sudden "HEY! "
we're jumping up and losing track
 because Rune struck again - okay!

A hop, a smoke, a lightning from the side
nobody sees that coming, nope
We'll get up and laugh right away
because that's how Rune is - every eternal road

(Verse 4)
He is a heart warrior in the circle
asking questions only in love
cutting fear and bullshit away
so we can stand in honesty
He swinging heart hammer in the field
bang - then games and talk fall
and in the midst of all that crumbling around
Rune stands calm, rank and straight

(Bridge)
1-3-7 and also 1-1-7
these are numbers we know well
The Love Charge is filling the room
When Rune says what was supposed to be said
He will balance, will equalize
no above, no behind
just people in real meeting
Day by day and blow by blow

(Surrender - sing along)
For Rune took an IQ test
it said 69 - no stress at all
he's not smart about numbers and shit
he is wise - in the good old way
He laughs at rules, breaks system
see some truth in there

(Shout Out / Sing Along)
He's an idiot!
- or just as clever
(haha!)
He's an idiot!
- in the right way yes
For he is wise
in the good old fashioned way
Yes, Rune is wise
in the good old fashioned way

Chance of Change
by Rune Darling

A SOUL CHANGE
IN AMNIOTIC
PLASMA FLUID

.

Souls Of
Serapeum
Passing On

.

The Old You
Is Constantly
Coming To An End

.

The Future's In The Air
The New Now **Already Here**
Can You Sense It Everywhere

.

Together **WE** ARE
Water Of Change

.

This Night Souls
Of 9 Descends
In The WaterFlow
Of 1 Chance of Change

.

Love And Trust In Harmony
The Magic Of The Moment

.

Listen To The Water
Flows Straight Into Air
Like A Water Flux
Only Now Will Take Us There

.

RING THE FREEDOM BELL
FOR PEACE OF MIND

.

#144
#137

01-Clock-10*

by Cheryl

**with credit given to Rune Darling*
for title inspiration and words in quotes

The portal of time
is opening--

The ancient Norse
call is heard in our blood.
"See the clock in the stars."

We straighten our backbones--
standing tall--
"Time is our space."

13 Stars now glimmer,
they've put on their glammer--
for the New Year's party.

The Earth aligns her backbone--
Axis--
Correcting the wrongs of a millennium.
Selah.

Reset.
The cosmic chronometer reads
01-01-01.

No more two--
Only one.

We are One
--with all--
Our time is eternity.

Falling
by Dmitriy Vasygan

A little boy decided to jump over the abyss.
Ran and jumped, when he flew, he looked down and was afraid.
In this fear, a memory was erased, and a new one was created
to create the illusion that there was no abyss.
When he reached the edge, he did not notice that he was already
at the edge and thought he was still standing on two legs, when
actually he was flying over the abyss.

**The moral of this story is that we create the abyss with fear and by facing our fears we can fly.*

Hot Potato
by Le'Vell Zimmerman

Accept the emotions...

Even the heavy illusory ideas that bring discomfort.
They are brought up to be examined, accepted, and
released in you returning back to a space of peace.

It's not wise to harbor them beloved.

Have you ever played the game "Hot potato"?
-333

Fly Free
by Cheryl

Round and Round
We go---

swirl, whirl, twirl

Take your turn.

I am the marble in the Roulette wheel---
Circling.

I am a pebble in the whirlpool.

Take your turn.

Turn dirt into pearls.

I Am a pearl.

Go thru the furnace---come out,
all shiny and new---
Phoenix.

Fly Free--
unencumbered by others ideas, expectations, demands.

"Don't throw your pearls to swine."

One's Own Odyssey: A Journey Inward
by Yvonne 'Greenie' Trafton

One's Own Memorable Odyssey, It's a whirlwind Journey Inward. Hang onto your hat gonna be a wild ride! Step into it, be joyful, you Gotta Dance Thru Life before Life dances on you.

Journeying Inward, Journeying Outward, Do the Hokey Pokey,
Do the Hokey Pokey, Shake it all about!

Do The Hokey Pokey:
Put right arm in, take right arm out. Put your right arm in and shake it all about. Do the Hokey Pokey and turn yourself around, that's what it's all about! Put your left foot in, put your left foot out, and shake it all about.
Do the Hokey Pokey and turn yourself around, that's what it's all about! Put your whole self in, take your whole self out, put your whole self in and shake it all about. Do the Hokey Pokey and you turn yourself around, that's what it's all about!
Chorus:
Do the Hokey Pokey, Do the Hokey Pokey, Do the Hokey Pokey
That's what it's all about!

About What? Put Yourself In, Put Your Whole Self In, and shake it all about. It's All About: (Being All-In) (The-Inward-Self-Journeying), A Self Odyssey of Discovery, and Hard Shadow Work! Do the Hokey Pokey and shake it all-about and Life goes full circle--It's a spiral, we live in a spiral, we learn in a spiral, everything goes in a Spiral. Life is Ups and Downs!

Have Healthy Boundaries, Boundaries or A-Bound all around, Life's Ups and Downs, Freedom, what is freedom anyway? "FREE FROM ONESELF" or freedom to explore self, self explorations, Self-Explore, Singing Freedom to Oneself, Being Free, Being In Your Essence, Gotta dance thru life, stop and smell the yellow flowers, get new intentions. Be free to self explore the inner journey's dance, in the dance do you lead or does life lead you?
Get out of the way! Get out of your own way!
Purest Perfection is being in your essence to self-essence, essence all about-

Hooray to be free, truly free, that extravagant.

Fulfill (Why/Your/My Mission)
Why I/You Incarnated here on Earth.
It's My Introspection Odyssey, It's My Own Odyssey A Journey Inward, MY LIFE! It's a Whirlwind Ride....I say (LIFE IS) an "E" Ticket (a reference to old Disneyland Ticket books) "E" Tickets were the Best Park Rides!
Remember to find the opportunities. Dance the Dance of Life, find the pink sprinkles, sprinkle it all about, do the Hokey Pokey, shake it all about. Stop to smell the yellow flowers. Life is (short) because we waste most of it! Life can change in the blink of an eye! Live your life to the fullest.

TO BE IN MY ESSENCE, TO LIVE IN MY ESSENCE is the Universal Law, My Birth-Right Please. LOOK AT WHAT STOPS ME, IT WOULD BE ME,it would be me that stops me! STOP IT!!! To get out of my own way. Listen to my High-Self! Have healthy boundaries with 'myself' and others.

May I BE HEART-CENTERED Always! The Heart is the Center to Everything, the heart is the key, the heart matters, matters of the heart always. Follow my High-Heart, the high heart is my compass! In Our World here on Earth (One Heart) and Billions of People!

Life is such an amazing illusion, everything is an illusion, illusion of self, illusion of others, illusion of what a family should be, illusion of what society tells me to be, the illusion of everything we see or (don't see) the invisible worlds and spaces, or "don't want to see", the elephant in the room.

ILLUSIONS OF WHAT LIFE IS. and of what life is (not), LIFE IS BITTER-SWEET, FULL OF TASTY MORSELS AND FULL OF SOUR LEMONS, and SALT RUBBED IN ONE'S WOUNDS, and WOUNDS OF SELF that hurt--What's my negative pleasure to stay in, what does NOT serve me, self-heal the wounds, give your gifts and become strong.

What will I speak this New Moon Night to "Grandmother Moon" on her New Gemini Moon Night? No false prophecy at the cemetery. I will look up at the moon and Speak, State What, My Authoritative Prayers to Thrive, My New Intentions, My New Dreams, My Goals, What to Achieve, For Grandmother's Gentle Help to Keep Me on My True Will's Path, The Moon's guidance in the moon-light of the darkness of night, also requesting the Holy Volcano Mount Shasta for her assistance with my intentions and prayers.
 Thank You Mount Shasta Volcano. AHO!

Regained Innocence

by Cody Ray Richardson

**Cody shared at an open mic how through writing he was able to unlock this trauma giving him a panoramic view of life.*

I sit in a place undivided
A Pinnacle of balance
I can't tell if it's over or just beginning
I am born again
He has died
I am not sure who I will be tomorrow
I am thankful for this new opportunity
In the same thought I see myself thinking
Why, then, that
The answer is no matter
The fact I can question is enough
I will go in as long as I want to
I have the same wonderment I did as a child
I remember the day I grew up
It was very specific
We had a knock on the door as we ate dinner
I was 8
We had 8 places on our octagonal table
Mom sat across from dad
My father faced West
My mother faced East
He was at 12 o'clock or position 1
She was at 6 o'clock or position 5
I can't remember the placement of my siblings
I'm pretty sure my younger and older brother were to my right
My three older sisters sat across from me
It was always the same growing up
Until I was eventually removed from sitting next to my mother
That's a story for another time

At the time,
I sat on the right of my mother at whatever o'clock that is,
or position four
Suddenly our dinner was interrupted by a very loud knock
Bang bang bang
And screaming
I was in the perfect position to make it there first
I ran to the door

the lady was at the door hysterical

She said a boy had been hit by a car
I thought nothing of it and ran back up to the table
I think I remember my brother making fun of the ambulance chasers as he called them. He said
"The whole neighborhood was running with plastic bags just to get a piece of the boy."
I said I guess the lady will need glasses now, now that she killed someone
Definitely failed her drivers test
We laughed as naive children do
Ha Ha Ha
Dumb kid got hit by an old lady....
When I was back at the table
I remember playing with a cup and hitting my hand
I had not fully comprehended the situation
I smashed my cup against my hand and laughed
An unknown amount of child time later the whole house was crying
Everyone started bawling their faces out
I had no idea what was going on
I knew without knowing
Something was very off
I felt something I had never felt before
Sheer terror of knowing something was wrong but not knowing what it was
Then the bishop of our church came
He explained my best friend had been killed
That was the day I grew up
I was very ashamed I had been making fun of the very person
I loved,
as he lay in blood outside of our house
The guilt was overwhelming
I had taught him to jump in front of cars
I used to do it all the time
I thought it was hilarious
They will stop I told him
Somehow it always worked for me
That day it didn't work
I remember I being upset earlier because he said he didn't want to play, then I was angry he had not invited me
I thought that maybe I could have stopped it
Maybe it could have been me instead
I had never felt such a range of emotions all at once
 Before that I was innocent

I had never judged myself
I had never judged others
All of sudden I hated myself
I hated everyone
Especially the bishop
Especially the fact they waited hours to tell me
Everyone knew before me and hid it from me
In child time it was infinite
They had broken my trust
All of them
All of my family
The whole neighborhood knew and didn't tell me
They let me play
They let me imagine I still had a best friend
He had a twin brother
Would they play the same game with him I wondered
Why not just tell me
God would want me to know
I knew things then, I had not remembered until now
Today, I am born again
I don't know why or how
I do know trauma made me who I was
Trauma has made me who I am now
I don't know who I will be tomorrow
Today, I am a child
I'm free
I'm good
I am God and always have been
I always will be
I am ripping off the mask I learned to wear that day
and perfected every day after
until now

I am innocent
My family is innocent
The neighborhood is innocent
You are innocent
You are all innocent
We are all innocent again

The Journey Continues ...
by Janine Savient

We are heart-centered beings, whose essence is pure love.
We are naturally, beings of truth and transparency.
Thriving in our truth, we are joy seekers, we love to discover the hidden gems found in any moment we are fully present in.

In our purest form, we have the 'innocence of the child', yet carry the wisdom of the ages within us. With deep curiosity, we love nothing more than to explore life, lifting the layers in every moment and finding the new aspects of ourselves and life that birth through every experience.

We are naturally communal beings, who deepen into the bonds of affection that grow when in connection with others who are in their own beautiful heart awareness.

It is also vitally important to our wellbeing to be in stillness, in silence with ourselves often, where we commune within the spaciousness of our Soul Self.

Nature feeds us on every level --
physically, emotionally, mentally and spiritually.
This is so, because we are nature. Every element of nature is found in us also. Now, as we bring change to this reality, through our deepening presence, remembering our truth, feeling our hearts respond, being guided by our inner knowing-- it is time to really step up and live honestly, in accordance with our feelings.

As we shake of the dust of the old world (mind) ways and we emerge into our heart's shine, we must live to honor love. Live in awe and respect of the power, the beauty, and the presence of nature. Live with a clear conscience in every moment.

Therefore, in every moment, at every choice point, before every action taken, ask, 'how would love do this'.
What action would love take here?
How would love respond to this?
As love, what can I do to support this moment, this person, this situation... myself?

Then, what feels right in your heart, do, say, be that.

This way, love does not stay conceptual, it becomes experiential and through having the experience, feeling that deeply, we can own it as our deep knowing.

We are leaving the thinking mind behind with its concepts and coming home into our natural way of being, feeling, loving.

Presence.

Many thanks to these contributors:

Elizabeth Carillo
Ember Coal
Xris Della Costa
Rune Darling
Linda Groszyk
Jennifer Hershelman
Chris Johns
Mary Krkljus
Kazi Ayaz Mahesar
Malte
Vivian Marie McIntosh
Shima Moore
Rene Moraida
Pradeep Nawarathna
Lillian Poe
Cody Ray Richardson
Janine Savient
Anna Scheving
Shivrael
Mercy Talley
Yvonne 'Greenie' Trafton
Dmitriy Vasygan
Laurie Story Vela
Cheryl Lunar Wind
Le'Vell Zimmerman

Author page--

Cheryl Lunar Wind lives in the Mount Shasta area in a little town called Weed. She is a practicer of Mayan cosmology, Lakota ceremony, Star Knowledge and the Universal Laws including the Law of One. Her hobbies are writing poetry, music, dance, drum circles and love for all life; plant, animal and crystal. Cheryl has been a guide and spiritual teacher for many years. Now she shares wit and wisdom through poetry, and has published poetry books; Know Your Way, We Are One, Follow the White Rabbit, Love Your Light, LIFE: Shared thru Poetry, Come to Mount Shasta: Sacred Path Poetry, We Are Light, Finding Our Way Home, We Are Forever, Handshake With the Divine, Grand Rising: A New Day Has Dawned, Star Messages: Codes to Sing, Dance and Live by, Return to Innocence, Bloom Like Nature: Live the Natural Way, Creativity Brings Peace: Create & Share Your Gifts, May Love Lead, The Eventful Flash: Bringing Solar Waves of Change, The Setting Sun, Crossroads of Change, Step Into New Earth, Blessings Beyond Belief-- I Am: We Are, I Love Life and Life Loves Me, Love & Loss, Ascension Flight 999, Earth Almanac 2025, and now From Darkness to Light: Finding Your Inner Child.

Testimonials---

"Cheryl's poetry is very inspiring--particularly the way she compares life with the forces of nature. There is a special element in her poems that opens my heart and fills my soul with divine possiblities."
Giovanna Taormina, Co-Founder, One Circle Foundation

"Cheryl's poems have helped me to uncover and honor my own hidden memories. The beauty of her spirit is evident in each tender, insightful passage."
Marguerite Lorimer, www.earthalive.com

"A rare collection filled with raw, courageous honesty. Thought provoking words that will stop you in your tracks."
Snow Thorner, ED Open Sky Gallery, Montague, California

"When wisdom, guidance, confirming comfort, ect. arrives to us humans--from beings with the perspective of other realms--it is a divine gift. Especially in the form of what we call poetry, and through a being with no agenda; Cheryl Lunar Wind simply shares what source gives her!"---Dragon Love (Thomas) Budde

www.ingramcontent.com/pod-product-compliance
Lightning Source LLC
LaVergne TN
LVHW010941110826
845149LV00013B/2702

* 9 7 9 8 9 9 8 8 9 7 1 5 3 *